You Should Read This Book!

by Mrs. Martino's class
with Tony Stead

capstone classroom

Fancy Nancy

review by Kennedy

Fancy Nancy is a great book!

One reason is that she dresses up her dog.

I also like when she talks fancy.

Fancy Nancy is a great book
to read!

marvelous

Clifford

review by Jaiden

I think *Clifford* is a wonderful book to read!

You will like it because Clifford is the best dog ever.

Clifford is kind to everybody.

I really think you should read this book.

This is
THE best book

If You Had Animal Teeth

review by Trevor

If You Had Animal Teeth is a great book!

One reason is because I like the shark teeth.

If You Had Animal Teeth is the best book to read to learn about animals.

Shark teeth

Which book would you like to read?